What are burnet moths?

Introduction

Burnet moths are attractive and easily recognised day-flying moths. They have beautiful, glossy black wings with a pattern of crimson spots. Their conspicuous, black antennae thicken at the ends and resemble slender clubs. Being so attractive burnet moths are often mistaken for butter-flies but actually belong to the moth family Zygaenidae, within the Lepidoptera (butterflies and moths).

Closely related to burnets are forester moths, which are also day-flying but are coloured plain green. Both are found all over the world, except in New Zealand. In Britain there are seven species of burnet moth and three of forester moth. Of these UK species, three are restricted solely to Scotland and one other to Scotland and western Ireland only. Because some species are very rare and sparsely distributed, we have a responsibility to conserve them.

Six-spot burnet moth

Colours and defence

Burnet moths' brilliantly contrasting colours are a warning to would-be predators that they are poisonous and, if their bodies are crushed, they give off cyanide in dangerous concentrations. The caterpillars of most of the species also have a warning pattern of yellow and black. Once it was thought that the cyanide came from the vetches that the caterpillars of many species eat: some vetches do contain cyanide. However, even caterpillars that feed on harmless vetches have cyanide, so they can obviously produce it themselves. The moths also ooze pungent smelling drops of fluid when attacked, making them an altogether unappetising meal, with a formidable armoury of defences. Even so, this is not always an infallible defence.

New Forest burnet moth

Occasionally, birds eat the moths or feed them to their chicks. Some spiders and bugs also prey on them. Caterpillars and pupae may also be eaten, perhaps by specialist predators or by ravenously hungry birds. Newly fledged birds may try attacking burnets, before they learn that crimson and black means danger. But, because all burnets look similar, one lesson serves to protect all the species and this reduces the overall loss of moths.

The bright yellow and black markings of the five-spot burnet caterpillar act as a warning to predators.

Burnet moth caterpillars act as hosts for the parasitic grubs of some wasps and flies. Some of these parasites, it has been shown, produce a substance called rhodanase, an enzyme which destroys the cyanide.

Narrow-bordered five-spot burnet moths nectaring on devil's – bit scabious.

Six-spot burnet moths mating.

Living in the sun

Burnet moths bask in the sunshine and feed from the nectar of flowers found in their chosen grassland habitats. Most burnets, other than the mountain species, prefer warm grassy hollows and hillsides containing an abundance of vetches, the food for all but two of the species' caterpillars. The moths come out in high summer and live in colonies, often clustering many to a flowerhead, making them both conspicuous and attractive.

Males emerge before the females and regularly attend the female cocoons, mating even before the female has expanded and dried her wings.

Six-spot burnet moth eggs

The female lays batches of yellow eggs, often on the underside of flat leaves, and the tiny caterpillars hatch after about 11 days and crawl off to find their food. They feed and grow rapidly, at first chewing the surface creating pale patches on the leaves, but later removing the whole leaf blade. The young caterpillars also enjoy basking in the sun, to keep warm and speed their digestion.

The caterpillars, after growing and shedding three or four skins, crawl down to a sheltered crevice and hibernate, only re-appearing in the spring when the sunshine is strong. Most then feed and grow again, shedding three more skins before spinning a papery, spindle-shaped or oval cocoon in which to pupate. Some of the species make these cocoons high on grass stems, where they sway in the wind, which seems to deter potential predators. Others hide them down in the vegetation. After two to three weeks the adults emerge and the life-cycle begins again. In Britain there is only ever one generation each year.

Six- spot burnet caterpillar

Slender Scotch larvae basking in the spring sun

Some of the caterpillars which emerge from hibernation moult their winter skin but then, instead of starting to feed, they return to a resting phase until the following year. This lack of activity is a deliberate dormant condition, called diapause, in which the caterpillar's metabolic rate is reduced to almost zero to conserve its energy stores. In this state it is unresponsive to outside conditions. In some species the trick is repeated for a second summer. One theory suggests that in cold, wet years, which could spell disaster for the sun-loving adults, this ability to become dormant ensures that some of the population will survive until the next year, which may be more favourable. Other theories suggest that diapause helps to prevent levels of parasitism building up too much in the whole population, or that in-breeding is reduced if only part of each brood emerge in any one year. This habit is unique amongst moths and may help the smallest populations to survive. In a poor year, when very few adults are seen, there may be many more caterpillars waiting to appear the following year.

A newly hatched six-spot burnet moth dries its wings by its cocoon.

Burnet Moths in Scotland

The six-spot burnet - *Zygaena filipendulae*

The six-spot burnet is Scotland's most widespread species. It favours dune grasslands and rich meadows. In England this species occurs almost everywhere inland and it may be that in Scotland it is mainly coastal because this is where the climate is warmest.

Adult six-spot burnet moths feed on rosebay willowherb nectar.

The moth is easily recognised by its six crimson spots on each forewing, counting separately the two that are close together at the base of the wing. It is extremely abundant in grassy hollows in sand dunes, especially when it flocks to feed on the nectar of rosebay willowherb. This species is the most frequently seen burnet moth and is often mistaken for a butterfly.

Six-spot burnet moth

The caterpillar is creamy-yellow, with a series of black spots along the sides and back. Like all burnet moth caterpillars it is rather slug-shaped, with a hunched front and back end, but its colour makes it attractive as it feeds in the sunshine. The cocoons can be found high on marram grass stems and are yellow-white in colour. When the adults emerge they leave the black pupal case fragments sticking out of the upper end of the cocoon.

The six-spot burnet moth is the most frequently seen burnet moth, often being mistaken for a butterfly.

The narrow-bordered five-spot burnet has recently begun to invade Scotland's border counties.

The narrow-bordered five-spot burnet - *Zygaena lonicerae*

The narrow-bordered five-spot burnet, which lacks the outer sixth spot of the six-spot burnet, is widespread in England. In recent years it has begun to invade Scotland's border counties, spreading on rough grassland along road verges, railway lines and coasts.

Its caterpillars and cocoons are similar to those of the six-spot burnet, except that the caterpillars have sparse long white hairs, which are especially noticeable when covered with dew in the morning. Their cocoons are pure white, without any hint of yellow.

Adult narrow-bordered five-spot burnet moth (Skye race).

There is an entirely isolated race of this species found only on the south-west facing coast of Skye, living on the ungrazed grassland of the undercliff. Moths from this location are inclined to have larger crimson spots, which may even merge together.

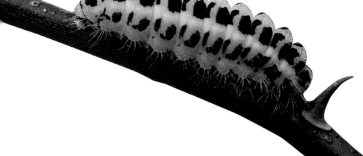

Five-spot burnet caterpillar

*Transparent
burnet moths*

The transparent burnet - *Zygaena purpuralis*

For many people this is the most striking and attractive of the burnet moths. The spots are replaced with crimson streaks of colour, set against an almost transparent grey-black background.

The British stronghold of the species is the coast of western Scotland, on steep south facing slopes just above the sea. Colonies are found in western Ireland and until 1962 there were also a few in north Wales, near Abersoch.

The caterpillars of the transparent burnet are unusual: they feed on wild thyme (*Thymus praecox*) and are a rather dull green colour, with two rows of black dots and small bright yellow flecks on their sides. They favour thyme growing in sunny, but sheltered, hollows but only occur where the surrounding vegetation is very short. They also enjoy sun-bathing on dark patches of bare soil.

Transparent burnet caterpillar

Because the rather dull cocoon is usually hidden amongst the vegetation, it can be startling to find myriads of these moths emerging in June on a slope where previously there was no apparent sign of cocoons.

The slender Scotch burnet - *Zygaena loti*

The slender Scotch is the first burnet to appear each year. In Britain, this species has only ever been found on the Morvern peninsula - where it is now apparently extinct - and on the islands of Mull and Ulva. It is currently restricted to warm south-facing slopes and undercliffs, on short herb-rich grasslands and closely associated with basalt rocks. These slopes are often unstable so the moth is most common on the rock and soil slides, where plants spread thinly across the disturbed, dark soil. Slender Scotch burnets congregate on flowers in small but abundant colonies. Although this practice makes them appear common there has been a marked reduction in the number of sites where they occur.

Slender Scotch burnet moth

A typical slender Scotch burnet moth habitat on Mull.

The outer two spots of the adult slender Scotch burnet are fused into a rounded crescent. The females choose to lay their eggs on plants which have a lot of surrounding bare earth, preferably in sunny hollows. The caterpillars spend much time basking on the warm soil. They are a dull greyish-black in colour with small yellow and black spots. As with the transparent burnet, their cocoons are hidden amongst the vegetation.

The mountain burnet - *Zygaena exulans*

Mountain burnet moth

This is the only species of burnet moth found in the mountains. It seems to be confined to only two or three of the hills near Braemar, in Aberdeenshire, and at altitudes of about 800 metres. The adult moths have hairy bodies and five dull red spots on their black wings. Presumably this helps to keep them warm and active during cool, cloudy interludes. No-one knows why they are so localised: their caterpillar's foodplant, crowberry, is abundant and widespread on the hills. Perhaps there is an, as yet , unidentified climatic factor at work.

The caterpillars are almost black, with small yellow spots. They feed slowly in the cool mountain climate and consequently spend more than one summer feeding, before eventually spinning their thin oval cocoons low down in the vegetation. It is possible the pupae can also overwinter more than once; if one season is unusually cold and wet only a few adults may emerge, with most of the population resting over for a more favourable year.

The mountain burnet was discovered in Britain in 1871 and fortunately it seems to be just as common now as then.

Crowberry

The New Forest burnet - *Zygaena viciae*

The New Forest burnet is found on only one small site on the coast of Argyll. This is one of the most critically endangered moths in Britain. The species was originally discovered in 1869 in clearings of open woodland and on the edge of heathlands in the New Forest, Hampshire. However, by 1927 habitat changes and over-collecting led to its decline and eventual extinction on the Hampshire site. It was thought to be extinct in the UK until the Argyll site was found in 1963. Here it inhabits a warm, grassy, coastal slope. Now it is very much restricted to one small part of this site and in recent years the population has dropped to around twenty adults.

New Forest burnet moth

New Forest burnet cocoon

The New Forest burnet moth caterpillar's foodplant, meadow vetchling, thrives in long vegetation, where it straggles up through tall grass stems. In the 1970s and early 1980s much of the site was heavily grazed and the vetchling gradually disappeared. Consequently, the moth became restricted to one ungrazed ledge, where it has survived in small and ever decreasing numbers. When, in 1991, it was realised this was the reason for the moth's rarity, a fence was erected which kept the sheep out and allowed the vegetation to recover. Immediately afterwards there was an increase in the numbers of flowers and the length of the grass. Although it is still too soon to be optimistic, the vetchling is re-colonising the site and there are signs the moth is beginning to spread beyond the ledge again.

The forester moth - *Adscita statices*

The forester moth is smaller and much less conspicuous than any of the burnet moths. It has plain, slightly metallic green wings and no contrasting spots. Its antennae are hardly thickened but the male has a series of prominent, comb-like projections called pectinations. Forester moths are found in damp meadows and coastal marshes. They are active throughout June, especially during sunny periods however unless the moths are sitting on flowers, taking nectar, they can be difficult to see.

Common sorrel

Forester moth

Forester moths lay their eggs in small batches on common sorrel, their foodplant. The caterpillars feed in two stages. Firstly, they burrow into the leaves, mining them as they eat. They then re-appear and continue feeding exposed on the lower leaves. Their feeding begins in July, overwintering once they are half-grown, before pupating in a loosely spun silk cocoon placed amongst the grass bases the following May.

Male forester moths use their feathered antennae to find their mates.

Table 1

The burnet and forester moths of Scotland

Species	Distribution	Status	Adult flight period	Foodplant of caterpillar
Six-spot burnet	Widespread on Scottish mainland coasts, some of Hebrides, and a few warm inland valleys	Generally common, abundant in places	July	Bird's foot trefoil (or greater bird's foot trefoil)
Five-spot burnet **Skye race**	Spreading into Scottish borders. Skye coast from Talisker to Glen Brittle	Common and increasing Stable	July	Meadow vetchling and other vetches and clovers
Transparent burnet	Coastal-from Skye, Mull and other Inner Hebrides; mainland near Oban and at SW tip of Kintyre	Declining markedly	Mid-June to July	Wild thyme
Slender Scotch burnet	Mull and Ulva only. (Extinct on Morvern)	Declining dramatically	Early June to early July	Bird's foot trefoil
Mountain burnet	Hills near Braemar only	Stable	July	Crowberry
New Forest burnet	One coastal site only in Argyll	Critically rare and endangered	July	Meadow vetchling
Forester moth	Coasts near Oban and in SW Scotland.	Perhaps declining	June.	Common sorrel

Six-spot burnet moth on wild thyme

Living in Isolation

Where did Scotland's burnet moths come from?

The colonies of burnet moths on the west coast of Scotland are very isolated from others of the same species and many people have wondered how they came to reach this location. Two separate theories have each had their champions. At first it was suggested that during the last Ice Age there was land, to the west of what is now the Scottish coast, that was free from ice and sufficiently temperate for moths to survive. By this theory, some burnets invaded Britain before the Ice Age, and formed a continuous distribution across the country. As the glaciers advanced this continuous population was split, with some colonies retreating southwards and some to the ice-free western fringe. Once the Ice Age began to give way to current milder climate these, now distinct, sub-populations re-invaded Britain and have remained separate ever since. It is now thought that during the last Ice Age there cannot have been any land to the west of Scotland that was sufficiently warm to act as a refuge, and that all burnets must have re-invaded from the south. The explanation for the current isolation of Scotland's burnets must therefore lie in the great climate variations that have taken place in Britain since the Ice Age. When the climate was warmer than it is now, there may well have been a more continuous distribution of these species and separation may have taken place as the present, slightly cooler, period developed. Perhaps the mountain burnet spread into Britain in the cool conditions which closely followed the retreat of the ice and climbed up into the Cairngorms as Britain's lowland climate became too warm for it.

Isolation and appearance

All of Scotland's isolated populations of burnet moth have developed slight, but consistent, differences in appearance from the main populations and are regarded, by some authorities, as distinct sub-species. For example, the five-spot burnet moths on Skye tend to be larger and to have more confluent spots than their English cousins. These Scottish populations therefore are specially important within the conservation of genetic diversity.

Many species have occasional specimens with the usual crimson spots replaced by yellow, brown or black. When studied these forms are found to be recessive to the usual crimson, although there may be a complex of genes involved. Some colonies, such as the transparent burnets on Skye, tend to have more of these colour forms than usual, which offer great scope for the analysis of genetic problems, particularly in relation to small, isolated populations.

On Skye an entirely isolated race of narrow-bordered five-spot burnet moths can be found.

Why are Scotland's burnets at risk of extinction?

It is probable the 'west coast' burnets are restricted to small colonies on especially sunny sites because of their need for warmth. In winter, such places will rarely have any frosts, whereas the inland valleys, which may have a hotter summer climate, will have more severe winters. Consequently they will always be found in rather small numbers in isolated coastal colonies, rather than having widespread and abundant populations.

Small isolated populations are particularly vulnerable to extinction. All insect populations tend to vary in size from year to year and a small population will tend to die out because of chance events more often than a larger one. Once the population from an isolated site has become extinct then the chance of re-colonisation from another population is low and a domino effect comes into play. Extinction on one site increases the isolation of the survivors elsewhere and makes their survival even less likely. This is the start of an 'extinction vortex'.

Six-spot burnet moth on sheepsbit scabious

Slender Scotch burnet cocoon

Small isolated populations will also contain only a proportion of the genetic make-up of the whole population, with less ability to adapt to changing conditions. If isolation is great, and occasional low numbers occur, then inbreeding will decrease the genetic complement even further. Recent work has shown that burnets do sometimes fly to nearby colonies, so re-mixing genes, but that this only happens when colonies are close together. Most of the burnet sites are now too far apart for this to occur.

When one of the few remaining populations of the rarer burnet species is threatened it is serious because any direct loss would diminish the survival chances of the remaining populations.

Changing habitats have led to declining burnet populations

The mountain burnet's habitat is largely unaffected by man and the moth's numbers have remained reasonably stable over the years. However, the transparent, slender Scotch and New Forest burnets have declined to a perilous degree. This is because man's treatment of their sites has changed, threatening the conditions they need to thrive.

Table 2
Threats to Scotland's burnets caused by changes to their habitat.

Threats	Species affected
Overgrazing causing reduction in sward height	New Forest burnet
Reduction in grazing causing increase in sward height and bracken invasion	Slender Scotch burnet Transparent burnet
Unknown threats	Forester
No known threats	Six-spot burnet Five-spot burnet Mountain burnet

Transparent burnet moths mating.

It is ironic that increased grazing has lead to the dramatic reduction of the New Forest burnet moth on its only known site, whereas it is reduced grazing that threatens the slender Scotch and transparent burnets. This clearly illustrates why the needs of each species must be researched separately. Now that these threats are known, proper management can be planned for the few remaining colonies of the most endangered species, in the hope that it is not too late! Perhaps, historical sites can also be returned to a suitable condition and re-establishments can be made, to try and build up population sizes and reduce isolation.

Conservation management for burnet moths

As well as the conservation action proposed below, continuing the search for new sites on unexplored parts of Scotland's west coast is vital, as is monitoring the numbers of the rarer species at their last colonies. Only by this monitoring will we know whether our conservation actions are succeeding.

Measuring the height of vegetation at a burnet moth site.

Species	Management required
New Forest burnet	• Persevere with reduced grazing; search for other colonies; consider establishing new colonies, once the existing one is secure.
Slender Scotch burnet	• Secure continued grazing on the current sites; re-establish grazing where this has declined; clear bracken where needed. • Search for new sites. • Consider restoring old sites and re-introducing colonies.
Transparent burnet	• Secure continued grazing on the current sites; re-establish grazing where this has declined. • Search for new sites.
Skye five-spot burnet	• No management needed. • Complete distribution survey. (Monitor spread into southern Scotland.)
Forester moth	• Complete distribution survey and assess status.
Mountain burnet	• Monitor occasionally to ensure continued survival at current status; continue survey for new sites.
Six-spot burnet	• No action needed at present; maintain awareness of general status.

Table 3
Conservation management for the rare burnet moths.

Burnets moths and the Law

Only the New Forest burnet moth has any legal protection at present. It is listed on Schedule 5 of the 1981 Wildlife and Conservation Act which makes it an offence to intentionally kill, injure, or take the moth, except under licence. It is also an offence to possess the moth, to sell the moth, to damage or destroy places which the moth uses for shelter and protection, or to disturb them in such a place.*

* This explanation should only be used as a guide to the law. For further details reference should be made to sections 9-11 and 16-27 of the Wildlife & Countryside Act.

Five-spot burnet moth

New Forest burnet caterpillar

The other burnet and forester moths do not have legal protection. None of them is faced with threats such as excessive collecting, so they would not necessarily benefit from protection under the Wildlife and Countryside Act. In fact, it is felt that such protection could be counter-productive: much of our knowledge of the distribution of these moths has come from amateur enthusiasts whose efforts might be restricted if the moths were protected. The level of protection of all of the burnets is, however, regularly assessed and the species are formally considered for protection at the five-yearly reviews of the schedules of the Wildlife & Countryside Act.

Transparent burnet moth

The Future

No-one can be optimistic about the survival of a moth like the New Forest burnet, which currently has an adult population of around 20 individuals, but there are a few signs that sensitive management is helping. There are still sufficient populations of the other species, however, for realistic management plans to be made, so there are grounds for some cautious optimism.

Scotland's burnets are a prize worth fighting for. Not only are they worth conserving for their own sake and for their beauty, but their exciting ability to use diapause to overcome climatic problems and their extraordinary defensive capabilities, make them especially interesting. Their isolation has led them to develop slight differences in appearance from other populations of the same species, so they represent a unique genetic resource.

Adult six-spot burnet moth

It is clear that we must act to ensure a secure future for Scotland's burnet moths.